THERE, THERE

There, there

Patrick Warner

SIGNAL EDITIONS IS AN IMPRINT OF VÉHICULE PRESS

Published with the generous assistance of The Canada Council for the
Arts and the Book Publishing Industry Development Program of the
Department of Canadian Heritage.

Signal Editions editor: Carmine Starnino
Cover design: David Drummond
Photograph of the author reprinted with permission of *The Telegram.*
Set in Minion by Simon Garamond
Printed by AGMV-Marquis Inc.

LIBRARY AND ARCHIVES CANADA CATALOGUING IN PUBLICATION DATA

Warner, Patrick, 1963
There, there / Patrick Warner.
Poems.
ISBN 1-55065-200-1

I. Title.

PS8595.A7756T44 2005   C811'.6   C2004-906575-0

Published by Véhicule Press, Montréal, Québec, Canada
www.vehiculepress.com

Distribution in Canada by LitDistCo
orders@lpg.ca

Distributed in the U.S. by Independent Publishers Group
www.ipgbook.com

Printed in Canada.

To three fine women:
Rochelle, Annie and Greta

Contents

ONE

TWO

Three

ONE

GUMSHOE

Packed in pick-up trucks they arrive at dawn,
these small, overalled, dark-skinned men,
from countries south of the Rio Grande,
who tend to the trees and bushes and lawns

in this mature suburban neighbourhood
where month-by-month nothing changes
except the flags, I mean the flags that flap
from slender dowels, that are set alongside

the tasselled poles that fly Old Glory,
silk flags set to mark a holiday or season,
pumpkins, shamrocks, hearts, and bunnies
signal the year-long consumer obsession,

in this neighbourhood where nobody walks,
where in places there are no sidewalks,
where no one seems to notice what I notice
when I walk, and there's no one to ask

about these inch-square zip-lock baggies
I find every morning, dew-fogged and stuck
to the pavement—what are these exactly,
sandwich bags for wee folk, for fairies?

Such folk myths belongs to the old countries,
to the Irish pubs down by the harbour,
to Germanytowns, Dutchlands, Little Italies.
New World folklore is of a different order.

Myths here are a poor man's collateral,
so new they don't seem like myths at all,
but swap stocks and bonds for gold and silver
and the city skyline for the magic kingdom,

and you'll understand why these lawns
are tended each day by Guatemalans,
Mexicans, El Salvadorians, Peruvians,
and you'll know why yesterday when I found

a sanitary napkin perched on the gutter
my first thought was of a magic slipper,
followed by thoughts of the ugly sisters,
and girls who will cut off their toes to fit in,

because that's the way it is in this place,
where the bloated frog is always the prince,
where there is blind belief in tomorrow
and in the wealth tomorrow will bring.

Today it brought a pair of black underwear,
women's black Moschino underwear,
dropped in the middle of an intersection
where I barely had time to examine them.

I thought, naturally, of Puss 'n Boots,
and maybe because I knew the ogre's fate
something a bit more sinister crept in,
and, as well, I was getting these looks

from a pair of Mexicans or Guatemalans,
both of whose faces barely topped
the four-foot hedge they were trimming,
faces right off a frieze in Tenochtitlán.

What's next, I wondered, a severed finger,
an arm, a ripped-out human heart,
a dead co-ed like Snow White on a lawn
surrounded by seven diminutive men?

Not that I'm saying it's all going to happen,
(as cases go it's not open and shut),
there are reasons the future is hidden,
but clues, too, if you know how to look.

MORMON

How will a Mormon boy get a wife, I wondered,
if he declines his mission to wander the world,
spreading the Mormon word as he goes:
no wife for a Mormon boy who refuses.

So I was kind to two young Mormon men
who came to my door last Saturday morning—
the point man in short-sleeved shirt and blue tie,
his back-up in short-sleeved shirt and blue tie—

the former displaying a pulp magazine
which featured a story on the fashion industry
and its dangers, especially to young women:
anorexia, bulimia, and low self-esteem.

I listened until—as if at some prearranged signal—
the second flipped open a leather-bound book
he had held until then with a sloth-like grip.
It was my cue to say: I am not a Christian.

This has been true of my life for so long
that to say it out loud gives only a moderate high,
which in turn brings only a moderate low.
And so I did not take it too badly on coming back in

to hear my eight-year-old daughter say,
in her deepest voice: *I am not a Christian*;
though to hear her say it brought it home in a new way,
and I thought for a moment that this is serious

and that she should take it more seriously,
so I considered putting the fear into her, telling her
that if her grandfather heard her say such a thing
he would think us condemned to eternal damnation.

Instead, I sat back down on the couch beside her
where it so happened there was scheduled
an end-of-season *Fashion File*—the year's best show,
the year's best designer, the year's best newcomer.

And watching, I reserved my loudest cheers
for headdresses of ostrich and emu feathers,
for models with bleached invisible eyebrows,
for models with slack, stew-bone thighs.

While she preferred the more womanly models—
though she did not care for naked breasts—
and reserved her loudest cheers for young Marc Jacobs
and for the ready-to-wear from Donna Karan.

What a world this is for a Mormon boy, I thought,
who declines his mission to wander the world,
spreading the Mormon word as he goes:
what a world for a Mormon boy who refuses.

HOT TURKEY

Mashed potatoes, fried onions, and gravy,
Brussels sprouts, turnips, sweet carrots,
and a generous helping of Parton's Butterball turkey.
Shortly after this, my 6000th dinner with you,
I lie down on the grey velour couch.

I drift uneasily to sleep, dimly aware
of the clash of crockery and kitchen utensils
as the routine mastications of a giant
who would grind my bones to make its bread,
spread my eyeball aspic on a Ritz.

Even so, I know that soon she will forgive me.
Had I the energy I would shout out to her
to come and sit in the white, Ikea recliner,
to come and watch how I peel away from myself
like one layer of semi-translucent onion,

to watch how that ghostly self hovers over
my sleeping self like a proud father, ready
to dart back at the first sign that I'm waking,
worried in case it does not make it back in time,
and, waking bereft, I set about ransacking

the world for something I can never find.
Come over now and join me sleeping here,
I want to say, let us cuddle close together
while our souls drift up around the ceiling
as in a painting by Mark Chagall.

Let sameness be the surprise we foist
upon the world, let us share 6000 more dinners,
let the lonely who wish to know our secret,
who peer through the yellow square of our
livingroom window, find us fast asleep.

CAPELIN

I

Where we lived over on the Southside Road,
our landlord and his wife both loved to garden.
Come-from-aways, as they say in Newfoundland,
neither seemed happy, and she was often gone.

She was shrill and had to get things done at once;
we guessed that she had long ago lost patience
with his absentmindedness and long silences,
suffering as he did from a growing rootlessness.

I remember one morning pulling back the drapes,
having got up from bed to investigate a noise,
and finding her bent double on the back steps,
wielding a can and a white emulsion brush,

bent so far over that her cotton dress rode up
above the backs of her knee-length nylons,
high enough to show off various varicose veins
and a swatch of her Tom Kitten knickers.

Did I mention that the landlord, one autumn,
tipping his hat to local practice—after forty years
of living as if he were still living in England—
ploughed into his garden a load of capelin?

II

Tonight, I am out with a friend on the razzle.
We are two men at the end of our twenties,
one whose wife is eight months pregnant
and one who has a daughter three months old.

Old friends, we have little to say to one another
as we watch the dance floor fogged in smoke.
We are glad of the music, the glare and sparkle
of the disco ball hanging high above us.

The dance floor heaves. It smells of grass,
deodorant and sweat, and something else—
a heady brew of bass and treble notes, a smell
designed to drive a man clean out of his mind.

Now my friend takes a mouthful of beer
and sprays the air above the dance floor.
An anthropologist will see in this a signal.
I watch it fall, a fine mist; I watch it touch

the skin of that one girl in silver spandex pants,
but my reverie is interrupted by speckle,
hot breath of sardines and fricative spittle
from this whale of a man at the rail beside me.

III

Late June, I watch the waves at Middle Cove
and imagine somewhere out there under fog
the capelin turn en masse toward the shore.
The beach rocks crackle, and every assault

brings another simile: a million castanets,
home-cut fries dumped in a deep-fat fryer,
wind-up dentures chattering on a table top,
a wound flushed out with hydrogen peroxide.

A ridge runs down the centre of the beach,
evidence of ice and more recent violent tides.
People wait with tin and plastic buckets,
with long handled dippers, and one tall man,

in hip rubbers, paces the wash like a stork,
an egret, a casting net draped from his arm.
All week, radio broadcasts called for capelin
runs along this stretch of shore, so far not here.

Out there, Humpbacks, Fin and Minkes blow.
Away from these the capelin school explodes
like cannoned ticker tape, a brilliant silver rush,
before they stall, turn inward, spangle.

BASILISK

What knows knows, but what knows this
is not what knows. What knows knew
enough last week to let me slump
and like some slow, dot-eyed tunneller
maw a bit-stream of low grade text.

I got nothing done, but work was done.
What knows knew that this week
I would need to up and, letting neck frill sail,
flare the water surface with a fringed foot,
turn the river skin to trampoline.

Lard tongue flicking, what knows sees
the black, soft mouth, slow-witted carp
bump its whiskers on the river bed
and knows that this is not
what knows, but reminds.

GENTLE

No you! No you! No you! he insisted.
You first! Me first? You first! Well then,
he said, and looked at me all falcon-eyed.
For a moment I felt like the very thing
he expected me to pluck
from the used margarine tub.
And seeing this he said, *Let me!*
And before I had time to contest,
he dipped four fingers and a thumb
into the flesh-fly larval squirm
and scattered these animate grains
across the surface of the lake.
And there he stood, mild as the reeds
that stork leg along the shallows
to the middle distance
where they thicken
to an illustrated cover
of *The Emperor's Green Son.*

OSSICLE

When ossicles hang by the wall
is no time to listen
it's time to let every hurt harden
every wound bleed and crust

it's time to scoop out the inside
of trust as if it were a pumpkin,
it's time to lie face down
and lovingly press your face in mud

it's time you understood
that leaving oneself behind
happens in geologic time,
think trilobite as imprint

think igneous and metamorphic
and rock-slab as library
and library as ossuary
and ossuary as primrose bouquet

where volcanic event is a hot date
where lava is love's outpouring
and building a future together
in the face of time

blue and perpetually fawning
our constant companion
not to be trusted
even on this summer day

where tides bubble between toes
and the carapaces of horseshoe crabs
like Halloween masks
litter the landwash.

MUD TROUT

I lean on the handrail and look down
to watch the waters deepen where the lock
to the shipyard dry-dock closes, turns
the river back. I watch the contrary currents
meet in a counterclockwise swirl around
the bridge piles just below my feet:
a soft ticker-tape of toilet tissue,
of knotted, reservoir-tipped condoms,
and bleached, freak-haired tampons.
I watch the river eat the shoreline
and climb the silvered shore piles
until the abandoned supermarket trolley
is submerged, and the white burlap sacks,
each tied at the neck, sway upward
from their anchor rocks. Gills filtering
all that filth, the mud trout thrive
in this sewer pipe and river confluence,
where tails and fins are instruments
of a compass sense like common sense—

FAUX PERCH PLUG-BAIT

The two-piece plastic
faux perch plug-bait
dangles behind his back,
like one big bohemian earring.

He looks toward the target,
somewhere out there,
past the water lily pallets
and fly-speckled periscopes.

Loose monofilament burns
the back of his hand,
makes a fraying sound,
like a bluebottle's wings

as if flies toward
where he wants it to go
and further still,
to splash up a tiara.

He watches the billowing line fall,
soft as an eyelash,
and the slack line corkscrew
across the surface.

There is nothing for him to do now
but wait,
and imagine that two-piece
plastic lure sinking,

broken-backed through effervescence,
attended by a coterie of minnows
that move around it
like a crown of thorns.

TORTOISE AT TORONTO ZOO

I saw a tortoise at Toronto Zoo
so massive its patterned shell removed,
upturned and filled with sparkling water
might have made a bath for infant twins.

I watched it heave its weight against its pen,
heave hard and hard again against the gate
whose post once split was now braced
by a metal belt that tightened on a screw.

The door, too, had buckled at its base,
blond wood splinters sprayed the earth floor
where the steel finger of the latch
had torn through the pit-prop post.

The bare earth floor beneath its legs
was not so much scooped out as flattened
into a depression from its pushing,
pestled down to a compact powder.

Its head with eyes closed was another leg,
though with eyes opened it resembled
Mother Theresa without her tea-towel veil,
Sir Alec Guinness and a Moray eel.

It had the look of one who had been doing
this a long time: it might have pushed
a block of stone from flat Nile boats
over logs toward the distant pyramids.

It heaved and heaved. Patient beyond my
comprehension, with something
of the mountain and the ocean in its shell,
something that immense, that unknowable.

LETTER TO A YOUNG MOTH

Stay away from the porch light!
The slats are littered with the dismembered dead,
and the porch rail is dusted with ash.

Fly away to the evergreen wood this night;
feel the wet cold of the spruce bark
and curlicues of moss where you alight.

Crack your wings against the white moon
in such a way that the Great Horned owl,
when it comes, will feed only on this symbol.

Likewise, arrange your wings as wafers
wedged in a dish of vanilla ice cream:
this will confuse the bats

who are always so far ahead in their thinking
that they will anticipate both the ice cream
and its radar-scrambling migraine.

Lastly, do not grieve that you are not a butterfly.
Be happy being the vested creature that you are,
common as snowflakes this summer night.

THE POSSUM

Never having seen one except
in a picture, I felt a timorous wonder

that gave way to concern
when it fell heavily from the culvert,

a concern made counterfeit
by the vigour with which it got to its feet

like a street fighter still full of fight,
though with its talcum pallor

and rolling, tentative gait, it was a prisoner
let out from confinement to exercise.

And I knew there must be a reason
for its banishment, but could not name one

as I watched it hobble over rubble,
trailing behind it a long naked tail.

TWO

CRIB

I cling to old ideas disguised as new,
ideas rooted in the prehistoric second when
the gazelle, craning her graceful neck for grass,
was speared with a chunk of chipped volcanic glass.

Ideas that can build a civilization: the plough,
the fallow field, the family farm, the well.
But such a deep well—looking all the way
down gives vertigo. Stick your head in,

it is dark and full of whispers, echoes.
What light there is comes from behind,
is packed down by the pummel of eyes
until you see at the end a glimmer,

and the question, then, is what you see:
a mirror in which appears a wild, unknown
possibly-dangerous-probably-the-same-
maybe-original-self you recognize.

Or whether this watery waver is really
water—a far-down ledge where boats dock
quietly late at night, and dark faces,
wearing bandannas, disembark.

THE BACON COMPANY OF IRELAND

Ramps, double-decked trucks, stink, lights,
shouts, kicks, electric prods, coconuts,
the workmen's high calypso as pigs run,
speed croquet over piss-shellacked,
shit-plastered floors, gully and drain scored.

Inside, no messing in mess, the point
driven home, mallet or stun gun sets
each one staggering, a modern dance
to the skull's high pitch—don't we know
that they are as intelligent as us?

Orchestral machinery kicks in. The
conveyor belt's dangling clefs, a score
into which their hoofs are hooked.
Hoisted, they perform one leg
inverted ballet that turns to opera
that turns again into modern dance
(the classical forms will not contain)
as they flex, wriggle, twist, gyrate
all the way to the conductor,
whose shiny baton slashes.

Plashing then like sustained applause
each is conveyed to the fiery furnace
(think Shadrach, Meshach, and Abednego
without a collective agreement)
to have golden bristles singed away.

Think of mother starting up a fry,
while at the same time trying to style her hair,
while trying to get the kids out of bed—
now see the children, passing slit-eyed
along the hallway, their lips curled in a smile,
their bodies limp as if they are still

in the deepest sleep, untroubled by
the shrieks that come from far away
(and that have always lived in dreams),
as they pass one-by-one into a room
of stainless steel and shining white tile.

THE PIG LYRIC

The news made him bleed like a stuck pig.
He had thought himself in pig,
about to drive his pigs to market,
from which he'd return on the pig's back,
nibbling pig in a blanket.

But he had made a pig's ear of it
by drawing pig on pork,
and now it was back to pig in the middle,
between please the pigs
and pigs might fly,
between pig in a poke
and in a pig's eye.

MAXIMUM LIFE

She worked in claims for *Maximum Life*.
Her specialty was accidental death:
Highways Division. Her name was Joy
and she lived up to it. Sorting sorrow
to one side allowed her to do good,
work in the face of much that was bad.

A great deal of living dealt with the bad—
this she knew from *Maximum Life*;
and, as knowledge goes, this was a good
piece to have. Like knowledge of death,
it should not load you with sorrow,
but deepen your hunger for joy.

And what compartment or part of joy
could possibly be construed as bad?
For Joy, joylessness meant only sorrow,
days and minutes of ordinary life,
days and minutes in the shadow of death,
and what in that existence was good?

Insurance, she knew, was of the good.
While a cashed claim did not bring joy,
it lent fortitude in the face of death,
it lent some hope in the face of life
when everything about it felt bad.
It gave the bereaved time to sorrow.

For always there was an end to sorrow.
And at its end was a shining good,
the profound sense of a deepened life,
and an increased capacity for joy:
so Joy made believe—it was too bad
that she knew nothing about death.

In thirty-six years no loved-one's death
had touched her. She felt no sorrow
as she sorted, searching out the bad,
looking to reject claims to the good.
Finding reason, she felt an abstract joy,
like justice served in the face of death.

Maximum Life would not be fooled by death,
nor Joy by the most abject sorrow.
Insurance claims were either good or bad.

THE BAKER

What is it that stops the baker from crawling
into his own oven to incinerate himself?
What prevents him from selling his shop?
There are always witches on the look-out
for ovens, cooling racks, trolleys, mixers.
The jeweler would gladly rent his storefront
and the grocer offer a fair price for his van.
Yeast. It is a yeast sense that tells him, No!
The routine that is killing him also saves him,
the routine followed by the sun and moon.
And he knows the juggler never drops a ball,
though sometimes the juggler conceals
them in his hands. Then, the baker feels
as if the universe has a grudge against him,
that death is just sitting to one side waiting,
watching for a day, not unlike this one,
when, without provocation, it will pounce.
The baker knows when he sees it coming
he will remember that he always expected it,
that all his life was a preparation for this.

The world by turns is a punch in the face,
a kick in the groin, curses spattering him,
a hand grabbing for his night-deposit bag,
a knee in his ribs and his ribs cracking
one-by-one until he decides to let go.
That was July 7, 1983. An ordinary night,
as he walked two streets to the bank.
But the world by turns is equally surprising:
a month later, a woman walked into his shop
and complimented his skill as a baker.
She spoke voluminously of his rye bread.
She wanted his dinner rolls by the dozen
and described them as heavenly pillows.
She compared him to the great bread makers
and mentioned names he had never heard.

She came again often and she lingered.
Her hair was the same colour as her eyes,
and both were the colour of molasses.

Once he would have seen her as a threat,
but somewhere his fear had worn thin.
Maybe it was the manner of her asking.
She spoke to him like someone from a novel,
her sentences crisp and rich and inviting.
Her words touched in him some inclination.
He saw in his mind a toy boat on a pond.
He saw it rock, but for no apparent reason,
(there was no breeze; its sail hung limp)
maybe a carp has passed underneath it.
And then behind him on the scorched lawn
he heard someone crumple up a paper bag.
He saw the trees stir, the toy yacht tack
a bit to one side and move swiftly along.
This was how he moved into her arms.

FANCICAL

In his younger days it was cock fights.
Now it's pigeons. Rooftop geraniums.
At night he stands on the tarred incline
and takes dictation from the heavens.

He has written a book on the subject:
how connecting the dots gives us letters,
the sun and the moon a reason,
the movement of clouds a method.

It would never hold up in court.
His geraniums would die in the wild.
His fastest pigeon would not win a race,
but this is hardly the point.

No wild flowers know such reds,
no railway-track pigeons such sheen,
no scholars such seminal insights.
Perception is gold, fool's gold

he hangs in ropes around his neck,
to go with his new-fangled, curious step,
both folksy and formal, lively,
a fanfare fandango.

The same could be said for his book;
its unusual binding of one
continuous interlaced ribbon
yields symmetry. His fane.

Though it's not a boisterous bluster
as he is no swaggering braggart;
but as binding to book is he,
one and the same with his dream.

HIKE

Water Street West

Water Street West: gauntlet of drunks
sinking fangs into Lysol cans.
Hooray for all the young people!
Pigeons tending to opalescent plumage,
bathing in gasoline-streaked pools.
The dry-dock and the Waterford River filled
with big skillet trout, tampons,
faeces, and bottle-nosed condoms.
Southside Rd., near Buckley's house,
let the climb begin. Now.
High-top soles draw in a million bits
of cartographic data. Lactic acid monks
inscribe filigreed contours
on bulging calves, thighs.

Back of the Brow

On this occipital bun, rock shrugs off
fibrous peat and rock-splitting roots.
The hot pine funk knocked down by sea breeze.
Freshwater Bay, aquamarine where
bleached white plastic bottle buoys
mark out lobster pots. From here
the rock breakwater's a necklace of spawn
holding back black lake water.
The rest's an easy walk. Oh sure.
A slippered slope of pine, with hand holds.
Chest-high ferns where live fellatio bears.
I peel a sprig of dog rose, walk
the undermined cliff path, watch
the swaying yellow snakes of
rope beneath the sparkle.

Freshwater Bay

After coming all that way, I'm mugged
by thugs: a band of lupines. Stunned,
I stagger off, a bee with pollen-heavy legs,
come back again, lean in closer,
on hearing from their puckered lips,
Come hither hiker, lean in closer,
admire us, imagine a bouquet.
Taken, I wrestle with a bunch of stalks.
The lance-point flowers stir, whiplash.
One blinds me with its perfumed tip,
one neatly tops my cigarette.
A fire starts in yellow growth;
I stamp it out.

Dusk, Near the Cape Spear Road

722-2222. I call up Jiffy on the cell.
Yis, I knows where it is. I wait. A plastic bag
bulges, snaps in the breeze,
snagged on a punk-topped spruce.
Look back. A furled stand of parasols
around the rusted, shot-pocked shell
of a car, the ground around it
littered with shards of amber.
Stop to wonder how it got there,
Fifty yards in from the road
down a two-abreast trail.
Look back. Run a sunburned arm
over soft, salt-sore lips, taste
flowers, pine, this place.

WATCHING THE OCEAN

You arrived that night in a shimmering slate-blue suit,
a linen rayon weave that still smelled of the factory,
and that, depending on how and where it rumpled,
showed a silver-whitish, semen, salt-lick sheen.

And all who dropped your name in conversation
as if they knew you, were suddenly quiet about it;
they could only watch how you moved from room
to room, restless in yourself but still at ease,

watch and wonder how—even as you grazed the buffet
for sea-salt chips and a foaming glass of 7UP—
you commanded such attention, reverence:
all felt in the presence of someone magnanimous.

But better from afar, you left each one you met
feeling smaller, undermined, like a bureaucrat
before sublimity, like a connoisseur of porn
reviewing videotapes of his daughter's delivery.

And even those who subscribed to the ideal,
who wished to be scoured of conceits, scattered
like crab claws, like lost bleach-bottle buoys
and massive main timbers on an isolated beach

found that they did not care for the experience.
Hence their tales of other nights and other parties,
of gale-force winds that blew without warning,
of houses left with not a stick unbroken.

THE LAPSE

I was doing voices from the Exorcist:
Can ya spare a quarter for an old altar boy, Father?
La plume de ma tante,
when I drifted off the road and hit a hydrant.

Let me describe that hydrant:
little Buddha,
its colour blood-on-fresh-snow red
until repainted by the city, new-pus yellow.

The hydrant, well-bolted to the pavement,
did not clatter down the hill,
nor was there a geyser
which furred at altitude to foxtails

before falling off as mist.
I could have backed away with my buckled fender,
flashing all who looked a dented chrome grin,
but I was bothered by a drop

drop of water from the short chain
that connects the heavy screw-on caps
to the hydrant's stumps:
that chain I feel compelled to call an epaulette.

Perhaps I cracked the main, I thought.
I should report it.
And thought then of Christmas night,
the crinkle pile of presents pushing back

the bone-dry branches of the pine
against the heater's element,
bringing the fire truck's blare and blue strobe,
bringing the fire captain in his big red suit.

It was for him I most worried.
The thought of his good father's face
as he turns the hydrant's valve
first one way and then the other;

then walks between flab hoses to the fire
to pick the flower-headed nozzle,
its steel flickering red and orange,
its O like a caroller's mouth at hymn's end.

I watch him bring it to his ear and listen,
as to a telephone
where the party on the other end
has left down the receiver.

Down that tube he hears a tap-tap,
receding. Then only distance,
in which, if he listens closely,
he can hear a measured breathing.

THREE

SOMETHING BETTER

Should I appreciate the beauty of this page
that darts to me like a courier of unknown gender,
wearing short pants, bearing this message,
what comes next is always better than what was.

The present moment is always hard to imagine,
as this blank page is to the living tree,
where the pulp machine and press are history,
history that never tires of hearing its name.

The here and now is nothing if not a dilemma
precipitated from all previous solutions,
which is not likely to be solved in the future.
What does it mean to wish for something better?

Should I give up thinking there's a pool
of infinite solitude, of silence, of sentience:
the one in which I accidentally dipped my toe—
even now I rock on ripples of that once.

Should I give up thinking that this moment
is the moment, that this chrome-legged, orange
leatherette chair is the chair—no wonder
I always find the praiseful so ridiculous.

As I mock them, so they mock me with prayer.
It's a rare day indeed when I do not feel it
blunder like a happy child into my thoughts,
crossing in through eight lanes of traffic

to whisper at me: *and what's to stop you going
out to find that something better—fear?
Is all this thinking there is something better
just another way of never living here?*

Summer, a southerly breeze lifts the ash tree's
powdered underside, and under that—sea sparkle
and God reclining in a bubble bath of cloud.
Nearer still, a girl slips off her bathing suit.

And suddenly I am unconvinced that this
moment will be any more the moment, that this
chrome-legged, orange leatherette chair will be
any more the chair for my not going over there.

The present and here have no real relation,
any more than a couple of Wild Turkey drinkers,
on their second flagon, belong to a fraternity
other than the hilarious Phi Beta Beta,

which is not to say the present and there
exist in any more substantive relation—
though the place where I and cloud and naked girl
map out with cries of there and there

and ugh... My spectacles slide off my nose.
The girl puts on her clothes. We kiss again,
but something is remiss. Is this kiss the best,
or do we think there's still a better kiss?

And so we kiss again for consolation. There.
And there. In that kiss I taste my desolation,
the present which darts to me like a courier
of unknown gender, bearing this message.

POEM BEGINNING WITH A LINE BY P.K. PAGE
RECALLED INCORRECTLY

And yes it was a desert of sorts
and a river too.
There were as many going as coming.
I was with those going.

And yet each of us felt alone
except for a couple of crazy ones who thought
the walking crowd was a library
and that time could be told from each face.

His face is midnight.
His a landscape lit by moonlight.
His face is teak.
His has wide elephant haunches.

Her face is clouds on a windy day,
and behind her face the blue that feels
like a teacup taken
from a cold cupboard.

His face says no time.
Her face says all the time.
I am not lonely like many of these.
I am lonely, yes, but not like these.

It is the slow deep river
that sounds like kissing, like
lovers behind paper walls undressing,
like children's secrets.

His face says I'm on break.
Her face starts as if I tossed my hair
and splattered her with rain.
His face says I want.

Her face says am I not beautiful?
Of all these, am I not the one?
His face looks at mine
as if it were a clock.

And for a moment there is a glimmer
of we are the same.

RIP

Where she had been was a puff of feathers,
as though pheasants and hens had exploded
the coop. The air was sharp with bream,
pike, perch, trout, salmon, eel, or the waft
of these from the inside of his creel,
woven from rushes, curved to fit a hip.

A rough stretch, that's all they thought it was,
her hunger like a scythe for standing grain,
for the last handful of hay in the field.
For this her spirit rose above the brim,
then fell under the strickle of his eye,
and together they became a thing
of no value, dissolute, worn-out horses.

A view from the top of the hill.
German girls swimming naked in the river.
A matchbox full of homegrown weed.
A double take.

Your coming back to ruffle my hair where I sit
dejectedly on the dog-haired mat.
Jokes about your bald head.
Jokes about your hair getting long.

That breathy voice so many women use
to say goodbye on the telephone,
even if it's a business call, it says
that everything (again) is left unsaid.

We will do much more the next time.
We will go places.
Anywhere but here. Find
an unexpected government cheque.

Mornings, when the desire to do
just to make things bearable
is miraculously absent
a green leaf will unfurl

through a pause in mid-phrase, in mid-
sentence, mid-way through the spiel
that begins each day with waking
and ends with sleep.

Weather fronts like amoebas.
Those stamped H
chase those stamped L
east across the weather map

NEAR FAFFLE, NEAR FAFF

They make fun of his faffle, his faff,
each one side of the metal crush,
one in kerchief, stripped to the waist,
his tan a false shirt-front
and ladies' long evening gloves.
One wears a clipped cigarette on his ear;
the sun a fag-end dropped behind hills.
Two hired hands shearing sheep,
dosing for foot-rot, fluke.
Tick, goes the metal gun against teeth.
The sheep manhandled unsheepishly bleat,
while farmhands mock
the landowner's trademark stutter.
Tick, goes the master's cane against skin.
Dusk at the field end where they work.
Dusk and still a dozen to go,
nerves like rope ends unraveling.
Dusk in the wood where I've spent
the day gathering sticks.

FELT

The General wields a bristle whitewash brush
with which he daubs the many woolly sheep,
the white and black-faced, shivering sheep,
fluorescent red, fluorescent blue, fluorescent red,

so he can see them on the hillside from the road
and watch their movements, direct his dogs
(who are no more than cheap textbook ideas)
when it's time to move his little flock. Bleating,

all go together, all go as one toward the gap,
bleating out their tongue-depressor tongues
and pressing perms in close together, as if
protecting something precious in their midst.

The best of who we are hides in among them:
that dag-end ewe who fought to save her lambs;
that plump and pretty ewe who lifts her tail,
not for every hard head, but for you alone.

These ones the General would have us wear
as fine felt hats, fiduciary symbols curled
like the ram's horns, of such dignified import
it makes it easy to say: *We are all this one.*

Life goes best for those who, day-in-day-out,
find the wherewithal to work this trick, who
place one fine felt hat upon another, who
wear each hat as if it is the only one.

This is the genius of the General. We need
him, if only to filter his cleverness through
our many stupidities, if only to embroider
his clarities through our many sensitivities,

if only to hear him clearly call our names
when a cumulus settles on the mountain top,
and the world too much resembles us
who graze together in the present tense.

We leave behind a seeming devastation.
Green yellow grasses cropped to the root
flecked with full stops colons sheared semi
colons tailless commas the scattered split

shot of exclamation nearby the scythe of
exclamation the question without a handle
whole lines shorn of grammatical marks
I may someday revisit and impose upon.

THE PIG NARRATIVE

How could he remember, how could he forget,
his stock that had fattened on little but lies,
his stock that would never make it to market.

And how they might have, had he heeded advice,
had he listened to sense: *to be both drawer*
and drawee, they said, *will earn only disgrace.*

Whom should he blame; should he blame his mother
who could not only conceive and bring
a child to term but raise it without a father?

What a mess, and now all his scheming
would not bring oysters, would not bring bacon.
But then, wasn't that the nature of dreaming.

The thing must be bought without inspection;
you must be one caught in the middle
between ironical disbelief and pious devotion,

conniving with mantras of please the pigs:
Oh Lord, abrade my will to finest sand,
search out my pride, blast my parts to slag,

send me as ballast to Van Diemen's Land;
en route let me double as litter for dogs
they are shipping to hunt the great wild

boar, first brought by Captain Cook. Mr. Boggs,
the First Mate, spends the whole time shaving
and rubbing oil into his muscled legs,

or leaning over the starboard railing fishing
for long snouted fish he calls wrasses and grunts;
these he barbecues on deck before washing

them down with home-brew lager. He wants,
he says, only to retire and grow pig face—
as if saying this makes him seem less ignorant.

I would have read his ignorance as disguise
had I known the morning we ran aground
that we were not lost but in the right place

and that there was nothing sinister or underhand
about it. Imagination is not navigation,
and Pig Island will serve as Van Diemen's Land;

a place between disbelief and devotion;
a place where we carve out a language
some will call nonsense, a devolution;

a place whose *modus operandi* is as much
to confound as enlighten; a place where
there is no poverty at all in being rich;

a curious place where it's winter in summer;
where horses gallop and jump, without
ever bringing their four legs together.

Mother, before when I blamed without doubt,
I can now only doubt why I blamed
and by this curious path walk into the light

of your presence again, the frightful calm
that trailed about you like the fragrance
of the Arum lily. To remember this is a balm,

which is a curse, because I remember that once
to cure a melancholy, on which I had fed
to bursting—my belly blue-white as a louse—

you laid your hand on the top of my head.
It was August; you wore a summer dress
the colour of a hog, or hickory nut,

which afterwards bore the imprint of my face.
There, there, you said. *There, there, my pet.*
Never repeat yourself. That's my advice.

A BOVINE MELANCHOLY

for Patricia Warner née Ivy Margaret Brown

Hunkered down behind the wall, I looked up;
a light wash clipped the fieldstone battlements.
I gripped my ash spear–stripped of bark and sticky—
and waited for my chance to up and scatter
Friesians, Herefords and girl-eyed Jerseys
that came to drink that greeny, insect water.

Mostly, I wanted to see fright enter them,
make them swivel hard their hundredweights
on dainty hooves, make them churn the pale
of cream-cheese mud around the water tank,
make them turn, white-eyed, and, with drool
stringing from their chin beards, run.

Empathetic, I look back on this with indolence,
with a bowel and bladder-voiding panic.
It is with their brown bottle-sauce eyes I see
myself stretch out along the tank's edge;
I smell their fresh cattle smell, their liquid
dung bejewelled with amber horseflies.

At a safe distance, they wait. One coughs
expectantly, and, not to disappoint, I dip
my hand, slide it gently over green slime walls
up under the tank's concrete casket lid,
locate the ball cock, push down hard until
the faucet rushes, bubbles nibble up my arm.

My mother warned me I was not to go there,
but that seemed neither here nor there to me
until I sloshed back home to find her waiting
by our front gate. She seemed to have
a sixth sense, a foreknowledge of my lapses
that was puzzling—although now I see

I often saw that same trance in her: evenings,
standing at the kitchen sink, wrist-deep
in suds, looking out over the half curtain
at a *John West* salmon sunset, at dusk falling,
at swift playing *Mustang* to swallow's *Zero*
as she hummed a tune from South Pacific.

Dusk deepens. The window turns half mirror.
Her hands go still. Her humming stops.
What are you thinking about, I want to say,
and go to her, rest my head against her hip.
What secret world is this that so enchants
and makes her suddenly a stranger to me.

I want to run over and tug at her print dress,
shatter whatever thought it is that makes
her smile so bittersweet. I want to jump up
shouting, *Bloody Mary is the girl I love*,
but *Shhh* is all I hear, and the hypnotic rush
of white water from the tank's faucet.

In that surface, I saw half my face reflected,
along with clouds that framed a clown's white wig,
a nest for rusted *Coke* and *Fanta* cans, for
furred bottles and rocks we rained down
on water beetles, or when we played cyclops
to the rowing water spider—all there

but not there as the water lisped and lisped,
until the whole rocked and overflowed:
until everything ahead that was blue
turned a shade less blue became green,
and everything behind that was green
turned a shade less green became blue.

A BOVINE MELANCHOLY (REMIX)

And everything ahead that was blue
turned a shade less blue
became green.

And everything behind that was green
turned a shade less green
became blue.

From windswept hummock and shale slope,
sheep stare down,
dumb-struck, proprietary,
their droppings everywhere.

Here exclamation's fan blade
finally broke free.
Here question mark's sickle, worn thin,
got hitched to a quarter-full moon.

Moo, you say, as if contemplating
a dessert: you who thought
to lick winter like an ice-cream,
you who thought never
would never break down.

SURPRISE   it did, and afterwards
repaired
like space
on the yellow velour of tundra.

BEAR

I am often mistaken for a clumsy, rude person.
I have been called an ape, a lout, a boor,
an oaf, lubber, yahoo, brute, a churl.
And while I laugh off these accusations,
list mightily against their drift,
they have, over time, produced an effect.
I have a tendency to undersell my assets
or to oversell myself in an effort not to,
and this has led to even greater clumsiness.

When I am feeling low about it all,
I come down from the mountain, drawn
by the twinkling lights of the lumber town.
I wander among outcasts, Indians
who perch on stripped-out rusted wrecks
drinking Wild Turkey from paper bags,
who greet me with savage irony
as a messenger of the Great Spirit.
Their problem and mine are one,
one the same in this wilderness
where wilderness preserved is made less.
Not one of us is extraordinary.
We are all bound up in this.

Endure, endure say the refrigerators,
upended, their doors torn off.
I feel, too, a certain sympathy with these.
My lips are like loose rubber seals,
my smell chemical and rank
when I wander from my tree-fall den
in the first days of spring, or false spring.

The front door keyhole winks.
I walk toward it, set the door ajar and lean
against the door jamb yawning.
My stomach rumbles. I am hungry

for something small, delicate and sweet,
but I'll settle for Bear Claws and a cup
of strong cappuccino, a view of the street.

A windowpane in No. 13 rattles,
as if someone in there slammed a door.
It was a feeling like this awoke me.
I look across, see in that rippled pool
a white pine telephone pole raised
like a gently silencing finger.
My eye grows wider, taking in the world.
The pear tree that will soon bear fruit
bears no responsibility.
Shhhh. This is a secret.

THE REUNION

The air was filled with clockworks
because all our talk was thinking
as we walked the gravel paths through woods
on the first few days of the reunion.

We were hoping to catch a glimpse of deer,
herds of Red and Fallow deer
breasting ferns and Queen Anne's lace
in the shade of government-planted pines.

The air was filled with dainty hooves
because all our talk was listening,
with all our selves and senses cogs
and flywheels in a single clock.

Whatever happened to that family clock,
the one that no one ever wound
that seemed to wind itself by going?
Perish the sentimental thought, I thought,

and thought instead of Auden, Plath,
but I would not say what I was thinking.
Instead, I made as if to stretch,
to sneak a peek at my wristwatch

and turned my head in time to see
a stag glide past on invisible tracks,
his rack of antlers raised above the thicket.
This, the wind-up squirrel in the cedar,

the hours waiting for the rain to stop,
the non-stop talk—though not what was said—
are all I remember of that time. These
and the clock's tick when talking stopped.

FRIGIDAIRE

Your iris pulsing marks your pleasure,
or disappointment, as you survey
my racks and crispers overflowing,
or my insides bare of everything
but condiments and a wizened radish.

But wait! Let us relish for a moment
the paradox of your expectation:
that you will always find in me
something you long ago depleted,
something you have not replenished.

THE HOWARD JOHNSON

Loneliness pours from the air conditioner,
making strange the voices in the hall
where a Coke can dropping rumbles
like a bowling ball, where the icemaker
dumps only jackpots in the plastic pail.

Everything about the place is unreal
and tips toward parody: take for example
the bible tucked in each bed-side table,
the pornography on in-house cable.
Hours spent here amount to nothing.

One only has to step outside, return
to find the king-size beds remade,
the pillows plumped, the curtains drawn,
the air conditioner turned on low,
the hand-print on the bathroom mirror

wiped away, the toy shampoos refilled,
the suckered, rubber bathmat rolled,
the nine denominations of facecloths
and towels folded and hanging on a rail,
the slips of scented soaps replaced,

all signs of one's activity erased.
It is less a home-away-from-home
than an environment of extremes,
where the weight of evidence leans
toward one's never having been.

Acknowledgements

Thanks and love to Rochelle for everything. Thanks to Carmine Starnino whose editorial skills revealed this book. Thanks also to the editors of the following publications in which some of these poems first appeared: *TickleAce, Books in Canada, The Malahat Review, The Danforth Review, Grain, The Sunday Telegram, Maisonneuve,* and *Backyards of Heaven: An Anthology of Newfoundland and Irish poetry.*

Signal
EDITIONS

Carmine Starnino, Editor
Michael Harris, Founding Editor

 Véhicule Press

www.vehiculepress.com